THINK LIKE A DETECTIVE

A Kid's Guide to Critical Thinking

by David Pakman

No part of this publication may be reproduced, stored in a retrieval system, or transmitted in any form or by any means—electronic, photocopying, recording, or otherwise—without prior written permission, except in the case of brief excerpts in critical reviews and articles.

All rights reserved.

Copyright © 2023 David Pakman

ISBN: 9798395930071

The author disclaims responsibility for adverse effects or consequences from the misapplication or injudicious use of the information contained in this book. Mention of resources and associations does not imply an endorsement.

"The important thing is not to stop questioning. Curiosity has its own reason for existing."

— Albert Einstein

Are you ready to use your brain to solve mysteries and uncover hidden secrets? We're about to embark on an exciting journey through the world of critical thinking!

Meet Daniel – he's a curious young boy who loves solving mysteries. Daniel needs your help to become a true detective and master of critical thinking!

Critical thinking is like having a secret superpower. It helps you solve problems by asking the right questions, finding evidence, and spotting lies. As you join Daniel on his adventures, you'll use your powers of observation, questioning, and reasoning to make sense of the world around you and solve problems that others thought were impossible!

One way we can use our critical thinking superpower is by asking good questions!

Daniel needs your help to solve a mystery – where should we start?

- Detectives need to be careful when they're asking questions – we'll need to be specific about what we ask so we don't get mixed up with the wrong information!

- Detectives ask lots of follow-up questions to get more details – we should stay curious by using "why" and "how" questions to help us understand more clearly!

- Detectives know what information they'll need in order to solve a mystery – we should take our time before asking questions and think about what we really want to know!

Let's give it a try and use our critical thinking superpower to solve a mystery by asking good questions!

Max says that aliens are coming from outer space! But before we get too worried, let's use our critical thinking superpower to figure out if it's true. Here are some questions we could ask:

- How does Max know about the aliens? Does he have any proof?

- Have any other people seen the aliens too, or is Max the only one?

- If the aliens are coming to visit, why haven't they arrived yet?

- Have there been any strange lights in the sky or other unusual things happening that might be connected to the aliens?

- Is Max just kidding around, or is he serious about the aliens?

By asking these questions and thinking about the answers, we can figure out if we should believe Max. It's important to use our brains and ask questions before believing everything we hear! If Max doesn't have good answers, then what he says might not be true. What would you ask Max?

Another way to use our critical thinking superpower is by looking for evidence! Evidence is like a clue – it helps us get a full picture. But without good clues, we might not be able to solve the mystery.

Cassie tells Daniel that there's hidden treasure from a shipwreck under the ocean! Where should we start looking for evidence?

- Was there really a shipwreck?

- Did the ship actually have any treasure?

- Did someone already collect the treasure?

- Is there any reason Cassie would lie to Daniel? How did Cassie hear about the shipwreck?

- Is there a map to the treasure? Can we trust it?

By following these tips, we can figure out if the treasure really exists and where to find it. Let's practice using our critical thinking superpower to find good evidence and uncover the truth!

Tucker says he saw a ghost in his bedroom last night! Before we get too scared, let's use our critical thinking skills to figure out if it's true. What is some evidence we could look for to check if Tucker really saw a ghost?

- Ask Tucker to tell us what he saw: We can ask him to tell us what the ghost looked like, what it did, and where it was.

- Look for clues in the room: We can look around Tucker's bedroom for anything unusual like scratches or footprints.

- Watch videos: We can check if there are any videos from cameras or phones that might have recorded something in Tucker's room.

- Ask an expert: We could ask a doctor or scientist what they think about Tucker's story. Do most scientists believe in ghosts?

- See if it happened before: We can ask people who lived in Tucker's house if they ever saw a ghost.

It's important to remember that just because someone said they saw a ghost, it doesn't mean it's true. We should look for all the evidence we can find and not decide if something is true until we have all the facts!

What kind of evidence would you look for?

Sometimes people say things like "bananas are the best tasting fruit," or "the sun is very hot." Sometimes the things people say are facts, and sometimes they are opinions. A fact is something we can verify, and an opinion is a personal belief. There's nothing wrong with having an opinion, but confusing fact and opinion can cause us to make the wrong choices, so it's important that we learn how to tell the difference!

Daniel needs your help! Are these facts or opinions?

- Summer is the best season

- 1 + 2 = 3

- Swimming is more fun than running

- The Earth is a planet that rotates around the sun

- Monkeys are mammals

- Ice cream is the best dessert

Let's practice using our critical thinking superpower to identify opinion and fact!

Marge says "everyone knows that people with freckles are more likely to steal!"

Before we believe her and start being scared of people with freckles, let's use our critical thinking skills to figure out if Marge is just making an assumption.

Here are some ways that we can figure out if Marge is making an assumption:

- Ask Marge where she got her information. Is it from a trustworthy source?

- Look for evidence to support Marge's claim. Is there research that shows a connection between freckles and stealing?

- Is Marge making any sense? Is it likely that freckles would be connected to stealing?

- Look for other explanations or points of view. Do other people have different ideas?

It is important to check if the things people tell us are true or not, and we can do this by looking for evidence. Our assumptions might be true, but we should always double check.

Sometimes, people say things that aren't true on purpose. That's called lying. Don't worry, because with your critical thinking superpower, you can get better at spotting when somebody is telling a lie!

Daniel is shopping for some new pillows, and the salesperson says "these pillows are made out of unicorn hair!" Daniel is pretty sure that the salesperson is lying. How can he be sure?

- Do unicorns exist?

- Does anyone else agree that the pillow is made of unicorn hair?

- Does the salesperson seem trustworthy?

- Does the salesperson have a reason to lie?

- Has the salesperson lied in the past?

By asking questions like these, we can try to figure out if the salesperson is telling the truth. Let's practice using our critical thinking superpower to identify more lies!

Ronald says that 1,000 people went to his birthday party, but in the pictures, it looks like only 50 people were there. Let's use our critical thinking superpower to figure out if Ronald is telling a lie!

Here are some things that we can ask Ronald:

- Are there pictures or videos that show 1,000 people at the party?

- Did anyone else at the party see 1,000 people there?

- Has Ronald lied before?

- Is it likely that 1,000 people would go to a birthday party?

Spotting lies isn't always easy. Don't be afraid to ask questions, and remember that it's always ok to ask for help!

Hurray! We've used our critical thinking superpower to ask good questions, gather evidence, and spot lies. Now we're ready to come to a conclusion. Not all conclusions are created equally – some conclusions are stronger than others. How do we know which conclusion is best?

A conclusion is like a building. some buildings are built with strong materials that can survive any storm. These buildings are like strong conclusions based on good evidence.

But if a building is constructed with weak materials, it can easily fall down. These buildings are like conclusions that are based on assumptions, lies, and bad evidence.

We can check whether a building is safe, and we can also check if our ideas are correct. We should listen to other people's thoughts and be ready to think about other explanations for the things we believe. Let's use our critical thinking superpower to take what we've learned and draw the best conclusions!

Daniel is trying to solve the mystery of who stole cookies from the kitchen. You have three suspects: Sara, Dylan, and Katie. You have all the evidence you need and now have to decide who stole the cookies.

- Sara was in the kitchen when the cookies went missing, but you know that Sara doesn't like cookies and prefers ice cream. Sara has no history of stealing and has no reason to steal the cookies.

- Dylan has cookie crumbs all over his shirt, but he was at the park with a friend when the cookies went missing. Dylan says his friend gave him a cookie at the park, but we don't know for sure.

- Katie was also in the kitchen when the cookies went missing, has crumbs all over her face, and has stolen in the past. When we asked her about the cookies, she got nervous and kept changing her story.

Based on this, what conclusion would you make and why? Remember, the strongest conclusion is based on the best evidence and makes the most sense!

We did it! Together, we solved mysteries that others thought impossible. With your critical thinking superpower, you can now ask the right questions, gather evidence, and detect lies like a true detective.

The adventure doesn't end here! The world is full of mysteries waiting to be solved. When things don't make sense, you now have the tools to uncover the truth!

Daniel's adventures may be done for now, but yours are just beginning. You can use the things you've learned with Daniel to be a better problem solver. We had a blast solving mysteries together. Let's do it again soon!

Made in United States
Troutdale, OR
07/07/2023

11040354R00026